Buster Books

DO ELEPHANTS Ever FORGET?

And OTHER Puzzling Questions ANSWERED

Fully revised and updated edition first published in Great Britain in 2019
by Buster Books, an imprint of Michael O'Mara Books Limited,
9 Lion Yard, Tremadoc Road, London SW4 7NQ

Material in this book previously appeared in *Do Elephants Ever Forget?*, published in 2007.

W www.mombooks.com/buster
f Buster Books
🐦 @BusterBooks

A CIP catalogue record for this book is available from the British Library.

ISBN: 978-1-78055-512-6

1 3 5 7 9 10 8 6 4 2

This book was printed in January 2019 by Leo Paper Products Ltd,
Heshan Astros Printing Limited, Xuantan Temple Industrial Zone,
Gulao Town, Heshan City, Guangdong Province, China.

Written by Guy Campbell
Illustrated by Paul Moran

Edited by Helen Brown and Philippa Wingate
With special thanks to Malcolm Dixon and Jenny Sykes
Cover design by John Bigwood
Designed by Janene Spencer

Contents

34 When will the sun stop burning?

35 Why don't we ride zebras?

37 Why are yawns so contagious?

39 What should I do if I'm marooned on a desert island?

42 Do dolphins talk to each other?

45 Is chocolate really bad for me?

48 How many species of animal are still undiscovered?

50 Is cracking my knuckles bad for me?

52 What would happen if a meteorite hit the earth?

56 Am I more likely to be eaten by a shark, a lion or a crocodile?

58 How long can I be dead and be brought back to life?

60 What is the rarest animal in the world?

63 Do twins have the same fingerprints?

65 Why don't polar bears move somewhere warmer?

68 What makes the noise of thunder?

70 What are shadows made of?

72 Which are smarter – cats or dogs?

75 Why is the stuff that tastes bad good for me?

77 Why do squirrels have bushy tails?

80 Are my dreams trying to tell me something?

84 How much room is there on earth for each person?

86 What colour are a zebra's stripes?

88 Why don't spiders stick to their own webs?

90 Why is the sky blue?

92 Could scientists ever bring dinosaurs back to life?

95 Why am I tired when I have just woken up?

98 How long could I live on nothing but cola?

100 How high can an elephant jump?

102 How does medicine make me feel better?

105 Is there life on other planets?

108 How do horses sleep standing up and not fall over?

 110 What's the worst smelling thing in the world?

113 If I could only eat one food forever, which should I choose?

 117 Which animal is the deadliest in the world?

119 What makes something funny?

 122 How do flies walk across a ceiling?

124 Which is the oldest animal in the world?

Will my eyeballs POP OUT if I sneeze with my eyes open?

You may have heard scary stories warning that if you keep your eyelids open while sneezing your eyeballs will fly out or your eardrums will burst.

Sneezes are powerful bodily reactions and really shouldn't be messed with. When you sneeze, air is forced out of your nose or mouth at up to 160 kilometres per hour. If you tried to stop a sneeze, by clamping your mouth shut and pinching your nose, you might force all that fast-moving air into your 'Eustachian' tubes (the passages that go from the back of your throat to the part of your ears called the middle ear). This could rupture your eardrums — causing acute pain and possibly, in extreme cases, deafness. Moreover, a sneeze carries germs, pollen or dust (which your body is trying to get rid of by sneezing). This might get into your middle ear and cause infection.

When you sneeze, your eyes close automatically. This is called a reflex action, because you don't do it consciously. The reason for this reflex action might be to stop your eyes bulging uncomfortably during the sneeze. It might be to protect your eyes from possible infection from sneezed germs. Alternatively, your eyes might shut because your facial muscles tense up in preparation for the upcoming explosion of air.

There are a few people who have managed to train themselves to keep their eyes open while sneezing, and their eyeballs don't pop out – honest. It is a difficult feat to perform, so you might ask why they bother. Well, here's one reason why it might be useful – if you were driving a racing car at 330 kilometres per hour, you could travel as far as 90 metres while your eyes were shut during a sneeze! Pretty dangerous.

Do ELEPHANTS ever FORGET?

To have a good memory you need to have a big brain and a lot of experiences. In which case, elephants certainly have the attributes needed to have an excellent memory.

Elephants have the largest brain of any land animal. An adult male African elephant's brain weighs about 5,000 grammes, which is massive if you compare it to an adult male human's brain which weighs about 1,400 grammes, and a cat's brain which weighs only around 30 grammes. As for experiences, elephants can live to the ripe old age of 70, which is plenty of time to store up a lot of useful information.

Elephants use their memories to survive. Their great size means they need large quantities of food and water. They must remember where these resources can be found at certain times of year. Elephants use 'paths' to remember how to reach their food sources. These paths are followed by herds for generations.

For instance, in India during the 1950s, a house was built over an elephant path. Every year the people who lived in the house had to fight off dozens of elephants who tried to walk right through the walls. One year the elephants actually knocked the house down to regain access to their path.

The elephants in a herd are usually female. Males tend to wander off by themselves. It is important for the herd's safety that the older females remember these males, and whether they are friendly or not. This enables them to mate to produce more young and to protect those young from possible danger.

Studies have shown that elephants can remember human beings, too. They can recognise an individual person, by sight or by scent, even when they have not met for decades.

There is even evidence that elephants can bear grudges against people. In 1929 in Texas, USA, Black Diamond, an elephant in a travelling circus, killed a woman. People found out that the previous year when the circus had visited town the woman had encouraged Black Diamond's trainer to run away from the circus. They suspected that the elephant had neither forgotten nor forgiven her.

Recently, some experts have suggested that elephants' memories are so vivid that traumas during their infancy can cause them long-term suffering. As a result, their personalities can change. Basically, they can turn into 'difficult teenagers'. For example, in the 1980s, in parts of Uganda, Africa, many elephants were slaughtered for their valuable ivory tusks. Some experts believe that, as a result, hooligan elephants have been terrorising road users and even attacking towns and villages in revenge attacks ever since.

Why can't I taste things PROPERLY when I hold my NOSE?

You were born with about 10,000 taste buds in your mouth. Most of these are found on the surface of your tongue, and can detect sweet, savoury, sour, bitter and salty flavours.

Each of the taste buds on your tongue contains very sensitive microscopic hair-like filaments. These identify what you are eating and send information about it to your brain. They help you to survive by identifying bad or poisonous foods before you swallow them.

However, to taste complex flavours, such as nut and raisin chocolate or pepperoni pizza, your body needs lots more information, and this is where your nose comes in. When you tuck into the cheesy-meaty-tomatoey-ness of a Deep Pan Supreme, you are actually smelling as well as tasting it.

It's not just your nose that gathers flavour information. There are receptors in your throat and even on the surface of your eyes that receive information, too. If you don't believe this, peel an onion and see how quickly your eyes begin to water.

If you hold your nose, you will stop air reaching some of these receptors. This air is carrying all those flavour clues that fill out the complicated description of what you are eating. As a result, the 'flavour picture' becomes more vague. You might be able to tell whether something is bitter, sweet, savoury, salty or sour, but anything much more complicated won't get through to your brain.

So pinch your nose and discover how hard it is for you to tell the difference between an apple and a pear, or even an apple and an onion. As for a Deep Pan Supreme, you might as well eat a slice of warm doormat!

Do CATS always land on their feet?

It is true that cats are remarkably skilled at correcting themselves in mid-air during a fall so that they land safely on the ground feet-first. Maybe this is why some people say that cats seem to have nine lives.

However, doesn't this make you wonder why, if it is so agile, a cat ever falls in the first place? A cat is a hunter and, as a result, excellent at climbing trees. It has curved claws which, as well as being useful weapons, are great for gripping things, climbing, running and changing direction quickly when chasing lunch — whether that lunch is a bird, a mouse or anything else that is tasty and running away. A cat is focused on its prey — so focused that it can occasionally tumble over, bump into things or even fall out of a tree. When this happens, a cat's claws can act as a safety feature — grabbing on to passing branches to stop or slow down the fall.

A cat living on the tenth floor of an apartment building can easily become distracted when chasing a moth or a fly around a balcony and it may fall over the edge. Modern buildings, unlike trees, tend to be made of smooth materials, such as glass and concrete, that are a lot harder to grab hold of in the event of a fall.

IS THAT THE END OF THE CAT?

Not necessarily. Vets in New York, USA, have discovered that cats falling from high-rise buildings have a remarkably good survival rate. The strange thing is that the survival rate actually gets better if cats fall from a height above six floors up!

WHY?

While falling, a cat twists its body into a position where its feet are pointing downwards and its legs are spread wide. Once it achieves this position, its body is acting a bit like a parachute. The cat stops accelerating and starts to relax, which helps it to absorb the impact on landing. For the record, a cat takes about one metre to turn itself the right way up when falling. Falls from heights greater than a metre often result in a cat landing feet first. Therefore, a cat falling from only one floor up is more likely to run out of time to turn, land awkwardly and hurt itself, than a cat falling from six floors up.

Records show that cats have fallen from over 30 floors up and lived. The parachute effect means that a cat will achieve a maximum speed of around 95 kilometres per hour – which is only about half the maximum speed a human being's body would reach if it fell from the same height.

This doesn't mean *all* cats live after a fall from 40 floors up. They don't. However, their instincts and their agility give them a good chance of surviving.

What will happen if ALL the ice in the world MELTS?

Currently 65% to 70% of the world's fresh water is ice, held in glaciers and giant ice sheets. As this ice melts, the water flows into seas and oceans, and water levels rise around the world.

BUT WHAT WILL HAPPEN IF ALL THE ICE MELTS?

Scientists overwhelmingly agree that Earth is getting warmer. Most scientists believe that the pollution human beings create is increasing the speed at which the planet is heating up. Glaciers and ice sheets are melting. Over the next century, it is estimated that most of the world's mountain glaciers will disappear. This is of immediate concern because the people and animals who live near them will suffer flooding and, when the glaciers are gone, they will lose valuable water supplies. However, the levels of the planet's oceans will only increase by less than one metre.

There is a huge amount of ice at the North and South Poles of the Earth. In the north is the Arctic – a huge ocean of ice. Some scientists estimate that a 2°C rise in water temperatures would be enough to melt much of the ice in the Arctic. They predict that in just 40 years there will be no ice over the North Pole at all during the warmer summer months. This would affect all sorts of things, including marine life and global weather. However, it would not lead to the land being flooded. Think of the Arctic ice like ice cubes in a glass of water. If the ice cubes melt, the level of the water remains the same. So if the Arctic turned from ice into water, the water level would stay pretty much the same.

At the South Pole is the continent of Antarctica. It is made up of a massive sheet of ice lying on top of land, above the level of the sea. If the ice of Antarctica melted, the water created would pour off the land and into the sea. This would raise water levels all around the world. The rise could be as much as 60 metres. As a result, vast areas of the world, including most of its major cities, would disappear under water.

Fortunately, the Antarctic ice lies on top of rocks, and the rising temperature of the ocean around these rocks will not affect the ice immediately. It would take a much greater global temperature rise of approximately 10°C or more to cause a serious melt. Currently, experts agree that Antarctica is unlikely to melt for tens of thousands of years.

The giant ice sheet that covers the island of Greenland is thought to be melting faster than the ice at the Antarctic. More than 200 cubic kilometres of ice is turning into water each year — imagine a cube 200 kilometres by 200 kilometres by 200 kilometres — that's huge. If the whole Greenland ice sheet melted, the sea levels might rise by around 7 metres. This rise would threaten low-lying coastal regions and cause serious flooding problems in cities like London, Amsterdam, New York, Miami, New Orleans, Sydney, Mumbai, Tokyo and Rio de Janeiro, to name but a few.

BUT DON'T PANIC

There are some indications that while some of the Greenland ice sheet is melting, other areas can at times of heavy snowfall get thicker.

Can a HEADLESS CHICKEN run around?

Have you ever been accused
of running around like a headless chicken –
making a lot of fuss but not getting anything done?
Surely a chicken without a head doesn't do
an awful lot of running around?

Some insects, including hardy cockroaches, can survive for weeks with no heads, but then cockroaches breathe through their bodies and can go for weeks without food. Chickens can't. Most chickens that are separated from their heads simply die.

This fact is what makes Mike the Headless Chicken so remarkable. In 1945, in Fruita, Colorado, USA, Mike the chicken had a date with the dinner table. Lloyd Olsen was given the job of finishing off the rooster with an axe so that his mum could serve Mike with potatoes and gravy.

By the time he died, Mike was famous around the world. He had lived for 18 months with no head – roosting, climbing and, of course, running around like a headless chicken. It appears that Lloyd had not done a great job chopping off Mike's head, and enough of the bird's brain stem (the part of the brain that runs down the neck connecting it to the spinal column) remained undamaged. This allowed Mike to pretty much carry on as normal.

Many people thought that the rumour of Mike's remarkable existence was a hoax. So Lloyd took the chicken to the University of Utah, and experts carried out a thorough examination. They confirmed that Mike was, indeed, headless — and moreover, he seemed happy.

Lloyd fed Mike milk and corn through the top of his neck with an eye-dropper. At the height of Mike's fame, Lloyd made around $5,000 a month showing him to paying visitors. Today Fruita still celebrates Mike the Headless Chicken Festival every year.

Next time someone says you are running around like a headless chicken, think of Mike and be proud.

Why can't I TICKLE myself?

If someone came up behind you and grabbed you, you would probably flinch or jump. This is because you have been taken by surprise and an area of your brain called the 'cerebellum' hasn't been able to warn you of the attack.

One of the many jobs your cerebellum has is to predict when something is going to touch you. However suddenly you try to grab yourself, you won't jump because your brain knows exactly where your hand is and what it is doing, and it anticipates the sensation of being grabbed.

This is the reason that you can't tickle yourself. Part of the helpless feeling that comes with being tickled is a result of not knowing exactly when and where the tickle is going to happen.

Tickling studies have been carried out by scientists. Robots were programmed to copy the movements of a person's hand, simultaneously and exactly. If a person wired up to the robot moved their hand forwards, the robot would move its hand forwards in exactly the same way and at exactly the same moment. Tests showed that if the person made the movement to tickle themselves and the robot tickled them at exactly the same time, the tickle didn't work. However, if there was a delay, even a small one, between the tickling movement and the robot's action, the person got tickled.

DOES THAT COUNT AS TICKLING YOURSELF? YOU DECIDE.

Why do KANGAROOS hop?

In the drier areas of Australia, kangaroos often need to travel great distances in search of food and water. During these journeys, it is important that they conserve as much energy as possible – so they hop.

Hops are useful to a kangaroo in other ways. The movement of the organs inside its body actually helps it to breathe. Air is pushed in and out of its lungs as it bounces along. As a result, a kangaroo uses less energy breathing when it is at full hop than it does when it is standing still.

Scientists have studied kangaroos in motion on powered treadmills. They discovered that over short distances kangaroos can cruise along at speeds of 40 kilometres per hour. At full sprint kangaroos can reach hopping speeds of up to 70 kilometres per hour – as fast as a racehorse. However, when they want to speed up, kangaroos don't increase the number of hops per minute by hopping faster. Instead, they make bigger hops.

For human beings, hopping is not a very efficient way of getting around – but kangaroos are in a different league when it comes to hopping. When landing from a hop, energy is stored in the large, stretchy tendons in a kangaroo's hind legs and tail. The tendons act like springs and release the energy again when the kangaroo takes off for the next hop.

When a kangaroo is hopping at full-speed it can cover a distance of 9 metres in one hop. There is an unconfirmed report that one particular kangaroo covered a distance of 13 metres in one hop.

The scientists' studies showed that this method of speeding up by increasing the length of a hop is extremely efficient. It requires a fraction of the energy increase other animals need to switch from a jog to a sprint.

Kangaroos have few natural predators, but the hop is a great way of avoiding pursuing hunters – it's not easy catching something that spends most of its time in the air and can clear rocks and rivers in a single bound.

WHAT A HOPPER!

How long could I SURVIVE by EATING MYSELF?

If you were stranded somewhere with no food, could you survive until you were rescued by chopping off one of your legs and eating it? It is not a very pleasant thought, but certain animals, such as insects, mice and sharks, have been known to eat bits of themselves when they are really hungry.

IS IT A GOOD IDEA?

Archaeologists have found evidence that suggesting that people who lived 100,000 years ago ate one another, and some believe this gruesome practice was widespread. This implies that there is nothing deadly or poisonous about eating human flesh.

But what about eating yourself? There are a few problems with lopping off a leg and eating it. First and most obviously, you wouldn't have a leg anymore. Second, the pain and shock of the injury might kill you. Moreover, your body might use up energy trying to heal the injury. In fact, your body would use as much energy healing the wound as it would gain from eating the leg.

You might think it would be a good idea to eat the parts of your body that you wouldn't miss and that would grow back, such as your hair or fingernails. The bad news is that there is very little energy-giving food to be had in these snacks. Nibbling the skin around your nails might provide a tiny bit of nourishment, but nothing you could really live on.

HOW ABOUT DRINKING YOUR OWN BLOOD?

Stories would have you believe that vampires drink blood, and some foods, such as black pudding, are actually made with animal blood. The problem with drinking your own blood is that blood is quite salty and drinking it will make you dehydrate (lose water in your body). In a survival situation, water is much more important to you than food. You can survive for weeks without food, but only a few days without water.

The reason you are so good at surviving without food is that after a couple of days without food your body starts to 'eat' itself. It uses itself as fuel. Your body begins to burn up reserves of fat and when that is gone it will burn muscle. This is by far the most efficient way of surviving by eating yourself – and you'll still have both legs free to go and look for the nearest supermarket.

When will the Sun STOP burning?

The Sun provides the Earth with warmth and light.
Without it, our planet would be just another frozen
rock flying through space, with no plants, animals
or people to make it the interesting place it is.

The Sun is a massive ball of gas. It gives off a huge amount
of light and heat. This energy is released when hydrogen gas
is turned into helium gas. This process is called fusion. It's a
fantastically efficient way of creating energy. Scientists hope
to use fusion to run power stations in years to come.

The Sun is thought to be around 4.5 billion years old. As it uses
up the hydrogen it contains, it will become bigger and brighter.
As it grows, the Sun will destroy the planet Mercury, and other
planets, including the Earth, will become burnt-out rocks.

How long will this take? Scientists think the Sun contains
enough hydrogen to carry on burning for another 4.5 billion
years. In one billion years the Earth may not be a place where
anyone would want to live – but then, a billion years is a very,
very long time.

EVEN YOU WON'T BE
AROUND THEN.

Why don't we ride ZEBRAS?

People have tried to tame and ride zebras for centuries. There are plenty of examples of zebras being trained to ride, pull carriages and even jump fences. However, the simple answer to the question 'Why don't we ride zebras?' is that they just don't like it.

Physically zebras are quite different from horses. Their backs are an awkward shape for a saddle. Their necks are strong but very stiff. They also don't have the same temperament as horses. They frighten easily, don't like doing what they are told, and they can be bad-tempered, even violent, on occasion.

In the 1900s, it became fashionable to use zebras to pull carts and carriages. On the plus side, they looked nice and were not affected by some of the diseases that killed mules and horses (most notably a disease called 'nagana' which is carried by a fly called the tsetse fly). On the down side, they didn't have the strength or stamina of mules and while getting them to wear a harness was relatively simple, they generally took a lot longer to train.

Attempts to breed zebras with horses or donkeys have been successful. The results (called, naturally enough, zorses and zonkeys) were healthy, but as domestic working animals they were no more useful than normal horses and donkeys.

A film called *Racing Stripes* told the story of a zebra in a circus who dreamt of being a champion racehorse. Eleven real zebras were used in the making of the film and each was trained to perform different circus tricks. According to the film's animal handler, Steve Martin, zebras are a lot easier to train if you start when they are babies.

CAN A ZEBRA RUN FASTER THAN A HORSE?

Well, a zebra can reach speeds of up to 60 kilometres per hour in a shortish sprint (particularly if it is being chased by a lion). Zebras are particularly good at changing direction at speed. However, over a longer distance, in a straight line, a horse would probably win.

Why are YAWNS so contagious?

It has probably happened to you – one hour into a long history lesson on a rainy Tuesday afternoon, someone yawns. Before you know it, the whole class is at it. Why?

The problem when answering this question is that no-one is really sure why yawns happen at all. One theory is that you yawn to wake yourself up and make yourself more alert.

You'll have noticed that you tend to yawn when you are sleepy (or bored in history lessons). Stretching and yawning increases your blood pressure and your heart rate, both of which make your body more alert. Moreover, your brain might decide you are feeling dopey because there is not enough oxygen in your blood – in which case taking in a big breath of air with a yawn would certainly seem a sensible thing to do.

If this is the case, yawns might be a very useful survival mechanism. After all, someone who is half asleep is more likely to be eaten by a polar bear than someone who is wide awake. This would then explain why yawns are contagious. When you watch other people yawn, your brain may subconsciously tell you that people around you are preparing to face danger and that you should probably start preparing, too – just in case.

Did you know that yawns are even contagious between different animals? (Try yawning in front of your cat – more than likely you will set him off.) In fact, yawns are so contagious that even looking at and thinking about the word 'yawn' can get you yawning.

WELL, HAS IT?

What should I do if I'm MAROONED on a DESERT ISLAND?

The obvious answer to the question 'What should I do if I'm marooned on a desert island?' is – get rescued. However it may take months and, though there are things you can do to make rescue more likely, your immediate problem is keeping yourself alive. You don't want to be just a skeleton lying on the beach when a helicopter does turn up.

The necessities for human survival are water, food, fire and shelter. You need all four to survive for any length of time. Believe it or not, a healthy human being can survive for over 40 days without food. Unfortunately, after a few days of missed meals, you will feel weak and find it difficult to think straight. Your body will become more vulnerable to diseases and less able to mend itself if injured. But you won't die.

Water is far more important than food. You can only survive about three days without it. The amount of water your body loses depends on how active you are and how hot you get, but it must be replaced or you will suffer dehydration, headaches, dizziness and confusion. Without water you will be pretty useless and eventually die.

You might think that on an island surrounded by an ocean, finding water wouldn't be a problem. However, any water you drink must be fresh, clean and free from salt, so drinking seawater is out. If you can't find fresh water on your island, rainwater will do. You can collect rainwater in a container or, failing that, use a piece of material to soak up dew from plants in the mornings.

A fire will keep you warm and keep dangerous animals at bay. More importantly, you can use it to boil any water that you find on the island. This will kill many of the things contaminating the water that could make you sick. You can also use your fire to cook any food you find. Another important function of your fire is to signal to ships and aircraft using its light and smoke.

Some specialists put building a shelter at the top of their list of things to do in a survival situation. A simple shelter that keeps you dry and protected from the Sun and the weather will enable you to sleep. This means you will conserve the energy you need to hunt and gather supplies and plan your escape.

Do dolphins TALK to each other?

Dolphins do communicate with each other. They use two kinds of sound signal, known by scientists as clicks and whistles. For the most part, these signals can't be heard by human beings, so scientists use special equipment to record and study them.

Dolphins appear to use clicks to locate objects. A dolphin sends out a loud click and hears an echo when it bounces off something. The echo gives the dolphin information about the location of the object and builds up a kind of 'sound map'. This technique is known as echolocation.

Dolphins appear to use whistles to identify other dolphins and call to them. Each dolphin seems to make his or her own personal whistle, like a unique signature. They can also imitate the whistles of other dolphins. They will imitate another dolphin's whistle to call out to it — a bit like shouting someone's name to get their attention.

A dolphin's signature whistle develops quite early in its life, and seems to be a close copy of its mother's personal whistle. So there is a resemblance between the whistles of family members. Scientists studying groups of dolphins (called pods) have discovered that dolphins can communicate the presence of danger, or the location of food. These messages can be passed from one dolphin to another, sometimes over great distances, so that everyone in the pod gets the news.

Scientists have also shown that dolphins can pass on more complicated messages. An experiment was set up in which a dolphin had to press a series of buttons in a particular sequence, using its nose, to release food – the dolphin was able to successfully communicate the correct sequence to another dolphin. Many trained dolphins can understand sign language, and some have been able to understand spoken words. Some experts believe that dolphins can even be trained to understand whole sentences, such as 'Hit the ball and then jump through the hoop.'

Some scientists think that dolphins have 'words' for things and use them to communicate with each other – it has even been suggested that one pod of dolphins might have a different language or accent to another pod.

No studies have yet proved that dolphins have actual conversations with each other, but the full range of their language skills is still being studied. More discoveries are being made all the time. Maybe one day scientists might be able to translate what dolphins are saying – and even talk back to them.

Is chocolate really BAD for me?

HAPPY EASTER

CRIME SCENE

Too much of anything is usually bad for you, and chocolate is no different. You probably know that eating chocolate all the time harms your teeth because of all the sugar it contains.

Chocolate contains a chemical called 'theobromine', which humans can digest safely. However many animals, especially cats and dogs, cannot digest it. Theobromine can stay in an animal's body for up to 20 hours and is poisonous. Even a small amount of chocolate, 50 grams or so, is extremely harmful to a dog or cat and could even kill them.

Theobromine is also harmful to babies and very young children. Their bodies are less able to process the chemical than the bodies of older kids and adults. That's one reason why small children who binge on chocolate get sick. So now you have the perfect excuse to take chocolate away from your kid brother or sister – you are being kind and merciful.

But chocolate is not all bad news ... there are over 300 known chemicals in chocolate, and some of them are actually good for you.

There are collections of chemicals in cocoa beans called 'flavonoids' that may help to stop clots forming in human blood and reduce the risk of heart attacks.

CHOCOLATE HAS BEEN FOUND TO HAVE A SOOTHING EFFECT ON COUGHS.

Scientists are investigating whether drugs made using cocoa beans could help people with diabetes. Chocolate contains ingredients that may make you feel happier by making your brain release mood-improving chemicals.

A little bit of pure, dark chocolate can make your skin better. Studies have shown that it is the fats in milk chocolate bars that cause spots, not the cocoa.

So could chocolate kill you? Well, if you ate enough chocolate in one go you might flood your body with enough toxins to cause fatal poisoning. The amount it would take to do this would be less if you are small rather than tall and much, much less if you are a cat … but don't worry, Kitty — any cat reading this book is probably clever enough to know that already.

How many SPECIES of animal are still undiscovered?

There are currently about one and a half million species of animal known to us. Different scientists give very different estimates of how many species remain undiscovered on our planet. Their estimates range from half a million to 50 million. The truth is that no one knows exactly how many species remain undiscovered.

A ten-year-long census of marine life recorded the diversity of life in the oceans. More than 2,700 scientists from 80 nations contributed to the census, and their research included 540 marine expeditions. These scientists reported their findings at The Royal Society, London, in October 2010 – they had found more than 1,200 new marine species!

Logging species in the oceans is one thing, but recording all the different insects on Earth is an altogether bigger task. Over half of all the species currently recorded are insects, including approximately 350,000 beetles. Some estimates put the total of different insect species at over 30 million, yet less than one million different species have been documented up to now.

Based on current research, it would be fair to say that a new species of fish is discovered about three times a week. But what about a new beetle? In the Amazon rainforest, pretty much anyone with a matchbox and a magnifying glass has a good chance of finding a new species of beetle before breakfast!

In comparison, only about 6,000 mammals are known to exist so, if a new one is discovered, you can't blame scientists for getting very excited.

Is CRACKING my knuckles bad for me?

Have you ever been told off for cracking your knuckles? Has someone winced and warned you that you are causing terrible damage to your hands? Perhaps you thought that the only reason they were complaining was because they hated the ghastly double-crunching noise your knuckles make?

The space between your finger bones in each of your knuckle joints is filled with a liquid called 'synovial fluid'. This helps to lubricate the joint and keep it working smoothly. Either side of the knuckle joint are ligaments — which are tough strings of tissue that hold your joints and bones together.

When you crack your knuckle joint, you are stretching the joint and making the space between your finger bones bigger. This causes bubbles of gas to form in the synovial fluid. The popping sound is caused by the bubbles popping.

IS CRACKING MY KNUCKLES ACTUALLY HARMFUL?

Well, joint injuries often involve tearing 'cartilage'. Cartilage is the tough, gristly tissue that forms a kind of cushion between bones. Cracking your knuckles puts the cartilage under some stress, but probably not enough to cause damage.

Studies on people who have been cracking their knuckles regularly for a long time show that they have slightly swollen knuckle joints compared to non-crackers. What is more concerning is that these people have a grip that is significantly weaker than it should be. This suggests that habitual knuckle-cracking might make your hands weaker over time.

SO IF YOU CRACK YOUR KNUCKLES – STOP NOW.

What would happen if a METEORITE hit the Earth?

A meteorite is a lump of rock, iron or other material flying through space. Millions enter the Earth's atmosphere every year, but most are so small that they burn away to nothing. Sometimes you will see them burning up – they are called shooting stars.

Dust from burned up meteorites is constantly falling to Earth, but the number of meteorites bigger than the size of a marble that survive the fiery fall is only about 500 per year.

The biggest meteorite ever found on Earth is the Hoba meteorite, which astronomers estimate landed 80,000 years ago in Namibia, Africa. A lot of the Hoba meteorite has rusted away since it landed on Earth, but it still weighs about 60 tonnes. Experts believe that the Earth's atmosphere slowed down the meteorite as it fell, so it landed pretty much in one piece and didn't cause a huge crater.

Few meteorites are big enough to cause a crater in the Earth's surface. However, if a very large meteorite entered our atmosphere, it wouldn't slow down much. It would thump into the ground at an incredible speed, at 50,000 kilometres per hour or faster. This would make a huge crater and kick up millions of tonnes of burning debris. The debris would set fire to anything it came into contact with.

The shockwave from the meteorite's impact flattens everything for miles around. The dust thrown into the air by the impact of the meteorite may also cause the sunlight to be blocked out for weeks or even years. If a meteorite this size landed in the ocean, it would create huge waves that would cause devastating floods in coastal areas.

Many scientists believe that a large meteorite (about 10 kilometres in diameter) smashing into the Earth killed off the dinosaurs millions of years ago. They think that a 180-kilometre-wide hole near the Mexican coast was caused by a massive impact. The hole is called the Chicxulub crater. Chicxulub is a Maya word meaning 'the tail of the devil'. The dust from the impact blocked out the Sun for many years. Plants stopped growing because of the lack of sunlight. This left nothing for the dinosaurs to eat and led to their extinction.

The good news is that a meteorite as big as the one that caused the Chicxulub crater only turns up about once every 100 million years. Another good thing is that the world's astronomers who study space would probably see it approaching Earth from a long way off. They are constantly searching the galaxy for giant meteorites on a collision course with our planet.

If astronomers did spot a meteorite that they calculated would collide with Earth in ten or twenty years' time, they would need to decide how to prevent this disaster. Different methods of doing this have been suggested. One way might be to nudge the meteorite off its collision course, either by attaching a huge sail to it or using the explosion of a nuclear weapon. This would be tricky, because meteorites are spinning all the time, making them hard to control. Also, a meteorite the size of Mount Everest would not be easy to push around.

Another method of preventing collision might be to blow the meteorite to pieces before it gets here. This is a risky idea, because the effect of millions of big rocks entering the planet's atmosphere could be almost as disastrous as the effect of one enormous one.

Am I more likely to be eaten by a SHARK, a LION or a CROCODILE?

The short answer to this question is that approximately ten people are killed by sharks each year, whereas as many as 700 people are killed by crocodiles, and about the same by lions and tigers. The difference is that crocodiles are the most likely to want to eat you.

The reason that fatal shark attacks are relatively few and far between may be because humans don't generally 'live' in the sea, so they don't bump into sharks very often. Of the approximately 400 species of sharks out there, only four or five are dangerous to humans. Sharks don't seem to hunt people on purpose. They are more likely to nibble people, mistaking them for big fishes or seals. They would probably stop once they realised. Unfortunately, a nibble from a shark is sometimes fatal, with people dying from the shock of the attack. In fact, sharks have much more to fear from humans, who kill millions of sharks every year.

Lions and tigers don't consider humans prey, and rarely seek them out for attack. Some people believe that an old or injured lion, unable to hunt its normal prey, will hunt people out of necessity. Once a lion has killed and eaten a human, it is likely he (and man-eating lions usually are male) will do it again. There have been cases of single lions or tigers that have developed a taste for people and have gone on to kill dozens, or even hundreds, over a period of years. In Tanzania, Africa, in the 1930s and 1940s, a pride of lions turned man-eaters and killed 1,500 people.

Crocodiles are different. Any croc big enough to attack and eat you will do it without a second thought. A crocodile's bite can be ten times more powerful than that of a big shark. They are 'ambush hunters' and hide themselves in water or behind a bush, waiting for something to wander up close. THEN THEY ATTACK.

How long can I be DEAD and be brought back to LIFE?

A person who is dead, whose heart has stopped beating, can be brought back to life. Their heart can sometimes be restarted by applying an electric shock, and their body can begin to function again.

If this 'resuscitation' happens within five minutes of someone's heart stopping, there is a good chance that they will make a full recovery. If a longer period of time passes (over eight minutes), a person's brain will have been deprived of oxygen and may well have suffered permanent damage.

Doctors have found that some people who have almost drowned in very cold water can make a good recovery, even if they have been under water for 30 minutes or more. Someone plunging into cold water experiences a 'diving response'. This means that their body reacts to the cold water by reducing the blood supply to the skin and muscles and supplying more blood to the heart and brain. As a result, these organs continue to receive vital oxygen for longer. The younger a person is, the better their chances are of surviving.

Cryonics is the practice of using extreme cold (minus 130°C) and chemicals to preserve the bodies of people who can't be kept alive by current medicine. The idea is that someone who has died of a disease, a medical condition or of old age, can be frozen and stored. Then at some time in the future, when medicine has progressed, it might be possible to defrost, resuscitate and cure them. Around the world, more than 300 people are currently being stored using cryonics, and thousands more have made arrangements to be preserved in this way.

No one has yet been brought back to life after being cryopreserved. It may be hundreds of years before medicine and technology are advanced enough to try.

What is the RAREST ANIMAL in the world?

The most endangered any animal can be is when only one example of it remains. Unless another creature of the same species (and of the opposite sex) comes along, that species is pretty much doomed to become extinct.

Thylacines, or Tasmanian tigers, have been officially extinct since 1936. These creatures actually looked more like stripy wild dogs than tigers. The last known thylacine, named Benjamin, died in Hobart Zoo on the island of Tasmania, Australia.

Benjamin (who may actually have been a female) remains the last one ever seen alive. Therefore, at that time, it could have been the only thylacine left in the world.

There have been investigations and expeditions, and a research and data centre was opened, dedicated to finding thylacines. Since Benjamin died, there have been over 300 reported sightings of thylacines, but none of them has ever been verified as genuine.

'Lonesome George' was a Pinta Island tortoise. In 1972, he was taken to live in the Galapagos Tortoise Breeding and Rearing Centre on Santa Cruz island in the Eastern Pacific Ocean. Until George was discovered, the species was thought to have been hunted to extinction.

The research scientists offered a reward to anyone who found a female Pinta Island tortoise. Sadly, they couldn't find one and, as George refused to mate with any other species of giant tortoise, when he died he was the last of his kind. In his last years, George was known as the world's rarest living creature, and was even named in *The Guinness Book of World Records.*

In 1997, a single male example of a newly discovered species of lizard, the Coromandel striped gecko, was found in the town of Coromandel, New Zealand. It was kept in captivity for four years, but died before anyone could find a female. A female was finally located and the search began for another male. Sadly, the female was attacked by a bird and passed away from her injuries, before a male was found.

In 2007, a male Coromandel striped gecko turned up, just 300 metres away from where the original gecko had been found. At that point, there were only three examples ever recorded. In the last ten years, conservationists have discovered more of these rare creatures, and while there is still a long way to go, it is thought that 32 Coromandel striped geckos are currently in existence today.

Do TWINS have the same fingerprints?

The difference between a pair of identical twins and a pair of non-identical twins is that the identical ones come from a single egg in their mother's womb. Non-identical ones come from separate eggs.

Non-identical twins are as similar to each other as brothers and sisters who are born at different times. They can have different coloured eyes or hair and won't necessarily look like each other at all.

Identical twins start out as pretty much the same person, because they come from the same egg. They have exactly the same biological and chemical make-up. Their eye and hair colour will be the same, and they tend to look very alike.

However, in the womb, once the egg that identical twins come from has split into two separate people, the twins can develop differently. Factors affect the babies in the womb that will lead to tiny differences developing before and after they are born.

These factors include if the babies lie in different positions, if they face in different directions and if they get different amounts of nourishment as they develop, which will cause them to grow at slightly different rates.

Identical twins might look very similar, but small details, such as the position of every hair on their heads and every freckle or mole on their bodies, vary.

Fingerprints fall into this category. A fingerprint is so detailed and complicated that each is unique to its owner. Even identical twins can be identified separately by their fingerprints, which will be similar, but not identical. So police at a crime scene would have little difficulty in telling which twin committed the crime ...

Why don't POLAR BEARS move somewhere warmer?

Polar bears are mainly found in cold regions near the North Pole, such as parts of Russia, Norway, Greenland, Canada and Alaska. They like to live by the sea, where the ice melts in the summer and freezes again in the winter, and where the seals they love to eat live.

Some scientists suspect that about a quarter of a million years ago, some brown bears may have been trapped in the far north by winter ice. In order to survive, the bears would probably have had to adapt themselves to their harsh new environment. These adaptations would have taken place gradually.

Over many generations, the bears grew bigger (today adult male polar bears measure 2.5 to 3.5 metres long and weigh 400 to 600 kilograms). Their legs became very powerful and their paws thickly furred to enable them to climb and run on snow and ice. Their claws and teeth grew longer and sharper so they could hunt prey and eat meat.

In their new environment, the bears needed to be excellent swimmers, so their necks grew longer and their paws became slightly webbed.

Today, polar bears have creamy-white fur which is excellent for camouflaging them in their snowy environment. Polar bears also have a thick layer of blubber beneath their skin to keep them warm. Which is just as well for creatures that have to survive in the harsh conditions of the Arctic, where winter temperatures can plunge to minus 45°C.

Polar bears are incredibly well suited to survive in the places they live. They are the most feared and effective predators in their part of the world. Polar bears have no real competition for food in the polar regions, and nothing is big enough and powerful enough to enjoy polar bears for dinner.

Moving to the warmer south might mean polar bears could live in a less harsh environment, but it would also mean living among other large predators, for example other bears, big cats, wolves and even crocodiles.

Polar bears would have to compete with these creatures for available food, and they would probably have to protect their cubs from them, too.

The characteristics that polar bears have developed to cope with the sea ice of their homeland are not suited to a warmer environment. Their creamy-white fur would make them so easy to spot that any prey would see them a long way off and have time to escape. This, of course, would make dinner very difficult to catch. Moreover, polar bears' long, flesh-tearing teeth are no longer any good for chewing plants.

So, although it might seem a good idea for polar bears to pack their bags and move to Florida, they really are better off where they live now. A barren landscape of ice and snow might seem pretty unpleasant, but for polar bears it's home sweet home.

What makes the noise of THUNDER?

Don't believe anyone who tells you the sound of thunder is caused by 'clouds bumping into each other'. Smile sympathetically and walk away.

Lightning strikes somewhere on Earth a hundred times every second. The huge release of electricity that occurs during a bolt of lightning heats the air around it to about 30,000°C. Heated air expands, and the air around the bolt becomes instantly squashed. As a result, the air pressure around the bolt increases a hundredfold, causing it to explode outwards, sending shock waves in all directions.

THIS IS WHAT MAKES THE BIG BOOMING NOISE.

Light travels more quickly than sound, so you will see the flash of lightning before you hear the thunder. A single vertical bolt of lightning will produce a single bang, but the shockwaves will reach you gradually, in one long rumble, starting with the ones near the ground which are nearest to you and ending with the ones coming at you from the top of the bolt.

Forked lightning consists of many different bolts, and the shockwaves from all the different strikes will bounce off each other and make low rumbling thunder that goes on for a long time.

Occasionally, no thunder accompanies a lightning bolt. This is thought to happen when a bolt travels more slowly than normal, giving the heated air around the bolt time to expand more gradually rather than exploding.

What are SHADOWS made of?

Light is a type of energy that makes it possible for us to see the world around us. Light comes from different sources such as the Sun, fire, stars and man-made things such as light bulbs and torches. Light rays travel from a source in straight lines, whether it's distant sunlight or light from a bedside lamp. Transparent objects (such as clear glass) let ALL light pass through them, whereas translucent objects (such as coloured glass) only allow SOME light to pass through.

Opaque objects, such as your own body, do not allow ANY light to pass through. On a sunny day, a dark area is formed behind you where the light can't reach, and this is called a shadow. It's not really 'made' of anything, it's simply the absence of direct light.

Shadows come in a variety of shapes and sizes, depending on the shape and size of the object causing the shadow. Something small like a mouse will make a small shadow and something big like a lion will make a big shadow. The biggest shadow we can experience on Earth is when the Moon passes in front of the Sun, known as a lunar eclipse, which plunges huge areas of land into an eerie darkness. The position of the Sun also affects the size of shadows, including your own. When the Sun is low in the sky you block more light, so your shadow is longer.

As the Earth turns and the Sun changes position in the sky, shadows move in the opposite direction. For centuries, people have used sundials rather than watches to tell the time, based on the way sunlight changes direction. The first device was the 'gnomon', dating from 3500 BCE. It was made of a vertical stick, and the length of the shadow it cast gave a sign of the time of day.

Shadows even exist in outer space, as they can occur anywhere there is a light source and an object to block it. Back on Earth, you can do loads of fun things with shadows. You could make a shadow frame using cardboard and experiment with translucent and opaque materials to investigate how the colour of shadows can change. You could also try to chase your own shadow.

DO YOU THINK YOU WOULD EVER CATCH IT?

Which are SMARTER — cats or dogs?

It's difficult to measure intelligence between one human being and another, let alone between two completely different species of animal. Different people have different skills – for example, a rocket scientist might be hopeless at writing poetry. So when answering the question 'Which are smarter – cats or dogs?' their different skills need to be considered.

Dogs are easier to train than cats. This is because they prefer to live in packs and have developed greater social skills than their feline friends. A pack of dogs must work together and communicate in order to hunt successfully. When you own a dog, it usually considers you the boss and itself a member of your pack. Therefore it will try to please you by doing what you tell it.

CATS DON'T REALLY CARE ABOUT PLEASING OTHERS.

They won't try to learn tricks just for your amusement and they naturally prefer to hunt alone. However, cats are better than dogs at solving problems, and at reasoning and learning by copying behaviour they see in others. Cats have been known to learn how to turn on taps, open cupboards and even use the toilet. But usually because the cat is thirsty, hungry or doesn't like the smell of poo! Cats are kind of selfish. This ability to learn by copying behaviour has been shown in monkeys and cats, but not so much in dogs.

Dogs can recognise signals and verbal commands given by their owners which help them become excellent sheep herders, rescue dogs, guard dogs, police dogs and guides for the blind. A dog's superior social skills also make it better at picking up on other forms of communication, such as a person's mood or body language. Some dogs seem able to detect illness – even undiagnosed cancer – in human beings.

Cats have been found to have greater navigational skills, and can remember what things look like longer than dogs. If you took a cat over 30 kilometres away from home and abandoned it, a week later it could well find its way home.

One approximate way to estimate the intelligence of an animal is to measure the weight of its brain in relation to its body. In the animal world, apes have the highest brain-to-body weight ratio, followed by whales and dolphins, and then by cats. Dogs come way down the list.

It's a close call. Suffice to say that a smart dog is smarter than a dumb cat and vice versa. For the record, poodles are usually smarter than Afghan hounds, and Siamese cats are usually smarter than Persian cats.

Why is the stuff that TASTES BAD good for me?

Don't you just hate the way that the stuff you like to eat, such as pizza, sweets and cheeseburgers, is usually bad for you, and the healthy foods — broccoli, liver and sprouts — taste awful? Have you ever asked yourself why you tend to like things that taste sweet or fatty — such as cheesecake and chips — and dislike stuff that tastes bitter, such as spinach or cabbage?

FOR HUNDREDS OF YEARS SCIENTISTS HAVE DIVIDED BASIC TASTES INTO SWEET, SOUR, SALTY AND BITTER.

A fifth taste called 'umami' was added around a hundred years ago. Umami is a kind of satisfying meaty-savoury taste. To survive, human beings need sugar, salt and protein in their diet, so maybe this is why they like the taste of sweet, salty and meaty foods.

In nature, sweetness (and sometimes sourness) is often a clue that a food can be eaten safely and contains good things, such as vitamin C. Bitterness, on the other hand, is sometimes an indication that a food is poisonous and should be avoided. Young children (and pregnant mothers) instinctively steer clear of bitter-tasting foods, perhaps for this very reason.

According to research, 'phytochemicals' found in some fruits and vegetables help your body combat diseases. Broccoli, cabbage and sprouts are particularly strong in this area, but many people don't like to eat them because they can have a bitter taste. Food scientists worked hard to breed these healthy vegetables to taste nicer, so kids would eat more of them, but discovered that the very phytochemicals that make them good at combatting disease also make them taste bitter! The sprouts that were bred to taste nicer turned out to have fewer of the good chemicals.

SO IN THIS CASE THE ANSWER IS YES – THE WORSE IT TASTES, THE BETTER IT IS FOR YOU!

Why do squirrels have BUSHY TAILS?

Squirrels are rodents, and come from the same animal family as rats and mice but, unlike these cousins, squirrels have big, bushy tails. There are many factors that make these tails more than just impressive fashion accessories.

Monkeys in trees use their tails for grabbing and swinging. Squirrels spend much of their time in trees but use their tails primarily to balance as they run along branches. When standing still on a branch, the tails act like tightrope walkers' poles, balancing with the squirrels' bodies and keeping them stable.

If squirrels are unlucky enough to fall, their tails act as a kind of parachute, slowing their descent and making for a softer landing. Even on the ground, the big, bushy tails act like rudders when the squirrels run, and help them to change direction at speed.

Squirrels' tails are as comfy and fluffy as they look. In the long winter months, when the temperature drops and food becomes more scarce, squirrels spend a lot of time curled up, using their tails as duvets, conserving heat and energy.

In the summer, squirrels can use their tails as protection from the Sun – indeed the word 'squirrel' derives from the Greek words 'skia', meaning shadow, and 'oura', meaning tail.

For defence, squirrels have some pretty impressive teeth to rely on, but their tails come in handy, too. Firstly, their tails double the size of the squirrels, making them look bigger and scarier than they actually are. Secondly, the squirrels shelter under their tails when on the ground, using them as fluffy barriers that protect their bodies from birds of prey attacking from the sky. The tails give the birds nothing solid to grab hold of and easily slip through their talons.

Most remarkably perhaps, squirrels have found a way of fending off rattlesnakes with their tails. Rattlesnakes use sensitive heat detectors on their heads to find prey. On encountering rattlesnakes, squirrels heat up their tails (which are usually cool) by filling them with blood. Faced with a hot, thrashing tail, most rattlesnakes back off and go elsewhere for lunch. Many scientists are convinced the squirrels' reaction is deliberate because, faced with other kinds of snakes that don't have heat sensors, they don't bother to heat up their tails. A specially constructed robot squirrel with a remote-controlled, heatable tail also proved effective at repelling a rattlesnake attack.

So, squirrels' tails turn out to be parasols, parachutes, rudders, balancing aids, duvets, shields and rattlesnake deterrents! Oh, and it makes them look cute, too ... when was the last time you saw a rat on a greetings card?

Are MY dreams trying to tell ME something?

People dream on average for two hours each night. Scientists aren't sure why, or even exactly where in the brain dreams come from. Nor has anyone proved whether dreams have any meaning.

Some experts believe that the subjects of our dreams reveal our deepest wishes and emotions. Other scientists think dreams are just random images and thoughts in our sleeping heads that the brain tries to make sense of by putting them into a story, and that they have no real meaning. Either way, it seems that the things you are dreaming about are important to you. If that is the case, maybe you should try to work out what you are trying to tell yourself.

'Oneirologists' is the name given to people who try to 'interpret' dreams, which means explain what they mean. Some dreams are common to lots of people, and there is a fair amount of agreement among oneirologists about what they might mean.

Being naked in a dream might mean that in real life you feel embarrassed about something, or that you have a secret you are worried about being revealed. Nakedness at school might suggest you don't feel prepared and are worried that people will find something out and make fun of you.

Falling is a sign that you feel insecure, out of control or that you've failed in some way. Often people will wake up with a jerk from a falling dream – but it certainly isn't true that if you hit the ground in your dream you will die in real life!

Exam dreams indicate that you are being measured or tested in some way. If the dream exam is going badly, it might mean that you feel you aren't fitting in or being accepted, or that you are worried about letting someone down.

Flying in a dream may indicate that you feel on top of things and are seeing things clearly — unless you are flying out of control, in which case it could mean that you are afraid of challenges, or even of success and the extra pressure that comes with it.

Losing teeth is a very common and upsetting dream, but it can mean simply that you are growing and maturing in life, losing your 'baby teeth' (or your childish ways).

Being chased in a dream might indicate that you are avoiding problems in your life, by running away from them rather than trying to solve them. The key to chase dreams is to work out what or who is chasing you. It might look like a lion, but it could be your geography homework, or that conversation you have to have with Dad about losing your phone ...

If you want to remember a dream, lie very still when you wake up and allow yourself to remember it. Keep a piece of paper by the bed so you can write it down.

Are dreams trying to tell you something? Well, yes. At the very least they are telling you about your emotions and worries, some of which you might have been hiding from yourself. Maybe you try to make sense of your world in dreams. Dream interpretation certainly can make you look at your problems in a new way, and sometimes that might be just what you need to do.

How much room is there on EARTH for each person?

Currently there are over 7.5 billion people on the Earth. If you looked at pictures of people on the streets of Hong Kong, New York or London you could be forgiven for thinking that the world is a pretty crowded place. However, there are still plenty of places on Earth, such as Canada and Greenland, where vast amounts of land are occupied by only a few people.

THE TOTAL SURFACE AREA OF EARTH IS 510 MILLION SQUARE KILOMETRES.

This works out at about 0.068 square kilometres for each of the seven and a half billion people on Earth. That's 68,000 square metres.

This might sound like quite a decent-sized piece of land. However, 70% of the Earth is covered in water, and a large proportion of the rest is covered in ice or desert. So these areas are not really somewhere people could live. Only about 10% of the Earth's surface can be successfully lived on. That is about 51 million square kilometres of habitable land. Divided between 7.5, that gives each person about 6,800 square metres.

SOME PEOPLE DON'T GET NEARLY THAT MUCH SPACE TO ROAM.

For example, the 38,000 people who live in Monaco (a tiny, crowded, but very wealthy country in the south of Europe) occupy on average just 59 square metres (bear in mind that's a square measuring less than 8 metres by 8 metres).

What COLOUR are a ZEBRA'S stripes?

There are three species of zebra, all with the familiar black-and-white-stripy thing going on.

The number of stripes ranges from 26 per side on a common zebra, up to 80 stripes per side on an imperial zebra. But are zebras black with white stripes, or white with black stripes? It's a question that has caused many a fight between otherwise perfectly polite zoologists.

The case for black animals with white stripes is convincing. Very occasionally zebras are born with spots instead of stripes. These spots are always white on a black background, so it seems logical that the stripes are also white on a black background.

AND THERE'S MORE ...

If you were to sneak up on a zebra while it was sleeping and shave off all its hair, the skin underneath would be black or dark brown.

WHITE

BLACK

BUT DON'T MAKE YOUR MIND UP YET ...

A zebra's black hairs are black because they contain cells that produce a dark pigment. When a baby zebra starts to grow inside its mother none of its hair cells produce this pigment, so it is completely white. The dark stripes only appear as the baby zebra grows, so it seems that the stripes are black on a white background.

Whichever side you're on, one thing everyone agrees is that zebras have stripes to protect them from hungry lions. Lions are colour-blind and the zebra's stripes make it difficult for lions to spot them amongst their natural habitat of tall grasses.

Why don't SPIDERS stick to their own WEBS?

All spiders make webs – some webs are big, some small, some neat and tidy, others completely messy. Not all spiderwebs are sticky. The ones that are sticky are made that way to trap insects for spiders to eat. A fly hits the web and becomes glued to it until the spider comes out and has it for lunch. But how can the spider move around on the web when the poor fly can't budge?

Spiderwebs are made from a substance commonly called silk. A spider can make different kinds of silk for different purposes. The silk it produces to wrap up eggs or to trap insects is different from the silk produced to make a web. Some silks are sticky and others are not.

To make a trapping web, a spider creates a web the shape of a bicycle wheel. First, a single strand of silk is attached between two twigs of a tree. Then a rim, like the tyre on a bicycle wheel, is spun in a circle around the outside, with a diameter the width of the space between the twigs. The 'spokes' are added next, followed by a loose spiral running from the centre of the web out to the rim. This forms the main structure of the web, and none of the silk used to make it is sticky.

Next, the spider weaves a second spiral over the web. This time the silk spun is coated with sticky stuff that flies will get trapped in. When the web is finished, the spider knows exactly which silk strands are sticky and which are not. It walks on the spokes, spiral and the rim of the web that aren't sticky, and avoids the spiral that is.

Why is the sky BLUE?

White light from the Sun is made up of a mixture of the colours you would see in a rainbow. All these colours are in the form of waves. The reddish colours have long wavelengths and bluish colours have shorter wavelengths.

The Earth's atmosphere contains atoms of nitrogen and oxygen. When light waves pass through it they are scattered by these atoms. The reddish waves are scattered least and the bluish light is scattered most. Therefore, most of the light that is scattered down to your eyes is bluish.

The Sun looks yellow to you because the light coming straight at your eyes from the Sun has lost some of its blue due to scattering. When the Sun sets and its light has to pass through more air to reach you, it changes from yellow to orange to red as more of the shorter wavelength blue and green light is scattered, and only the longer wavelength red light survives the journey to your eye.

The sky isn't always blue, though. Different weather and atmospheric conditions can make it appear different colours. It can sometimes look bright red. Particles of dust, water, volcanic ash or pollution in the air can all affect the way the light behaves and change the colour of the sky. The more particles there are in the air, the less of the short wavelength light makes it to your eye, and the redder the sky will appear.

Could scientists ever bring DINOSAURS back to life?

Wouldn't it be great to have your very own pet Triceratops stomping round the garden? Imagine how much stuff it could carry when you're coming back from shopping.

SCIENTISTS HAVE CLONED SHEEP AND CATS, SO WHY NOT DINOSAURS?

First, they would need some dinosaur DNA. DNA is the information contained in all the cells of an animal that provides instructions telling it what to look like as it grows. But how would they find the DNA of an extinct creature?

Ideally, one day, millions of years ago, a mosquito that had recently eaten some dinosaur blood for lunch would have become trapped in the sticky substance called resin that oozes out of trees. Tree resin is very good at preserving whatever becomes trapped in it for a long period of time. It's a bit like nature's cling film, only better.

Eventually the mosquito would become fossilised, as the resin hardened and became a substance called amber. If the scientists found the lump of amber and were able to extract dinosaur DNA from the blood inside the trapped mosquito, would they be able to use the DNA to bring dinosaurs back to life?

The main problem is that over very long periods of time the DNA does start to decay, like milk in a fridge. Bits of the DNA get lost or damaged — and you really need ALL of the information to be able to recreate a dinosaur.

Human beings share 70% of the same DNA with a slug, so you can see how important it is to have the whole thing.

YOU'D BE DISAPPOINTED IF YOU WERE TRYING TO GROW A HERD OF VELOCIRAPTORS AND ENDED UP WITH A MATCHBOX FULL OF EARWIGS ...

Also, over time, the DNA of the mosquito may well have become mixed up with the dinosaur's DNA, which might produce a huge mosquitosaurus, but is more likely to result in a big pile of green goo.

But here's the worst news. Even if scientists could get a complete set of dino-DNA, they would then need to get it to assemble into chromosomes and then use the chromosomes to fertilise an egg ... a live egg ... a live, dinosaur egg. This is probably an impossible task and, anyway, if they had a live dinosaur egg, why would scientists bother to clone a dinosaur in the first place?

Why am I tired when I have JUST woken up?

It seems reasonable to expect that after being awake all day, you should feel tired. It also seems reasonable to feel more awake after you have rested.

BUT SLEEPINESS ISN'T AS STRAIGHTFORWARD AS THAT.

Your body has an 'internal clock' which gives you a sense of time. For example, don't you find you often wake up just before your alarm rings in the morning? That is because of your body clock. But at certain times your internal clock doesn't work properly.

Research on very young children, babies and toddlers shows that the longer they are awake the sleepier they will be, just as you would expect. However, children aged between 10 and 12 years are likely to be less sleepy after 10 hours of being awake than after 5 hours. They will be even less sleepy after 14 hours.

The human body releases hormones that make it sleepy when it needs rest but, the age of about 10, and through the teenage years, the internal clock seems to delay doing this until later at night. This means teenagers often feel wide awake at about 9pm or 10pm, just when they should be feeling sleepy. This shift of the internal clock appears to go back to normal when people get older.

It is very common for teenagers to wake up feeling tired, have a sleepy period mid-afternoon, and to perk up at night. As a result, some sleep experts believe that the school day – starting in the early morning and ending mid-afternoon – is completely wrong for kids. Teens going to bed at midnight and getting up at seven o'clock in the morning are tired and unable to concentrate. This makes their memory poor and makes them less creative. Recent research shows it would be best to allow children to start their school day later.

So what can you do if you have trouble going to sleep at bedtime? Well, experts suggest that dimming the lights at night can help your body feel sleepier, and getting lots of daylight in the morning can wake you up. Don't 'binge sleep' at the weekend – get up just an hour or two later than normal, otherwise your internal clock becomes confused. Keep your bedroom cool, dark and quiet. Don't watch TV, surf the internet or listen to music right before you want to sleep. Also get some exercise, preferably early in the day.

Parents are often shocked when their lively kids – who used to get up at the crack of dawn full of energy – turn into lazy teenagers who can't get out of bed, yawn all day and still want to go out at night.

NOW YOU CAN EXPLAIN THAT IT SIMPLY ISN'T YOUR FAULT!

How long could I live on nothing but COLA?

The good news to anyone planning to live on cola alone is that it contains two of the things your body needs to survive – energy and water. This means that for the first few weeks of living on nothing but cola the worst of your problems would be sticky teeth and smelly breath.

THE BAD NEWS IS THAT COLA DOESN'T OFFER MUCH ELSE.

It doesn't contain any of the vitamins or minerals your body needs to function properly. Within a month of consuming nothing but cola, your hair would start to fall out, your nails would break easily and your skin would become scaly and start to flake off. The lack of a substance called 'fibre', which helps your body to poo, would mean you might spend hours sitting on the toilet clutching your stomach in agony.

Over a longer period of time the lack of essential substances called proteins in your diet would stop your brain from developing properly. It would stunt your growth and cause your muscles to waste away. Moreover, all the sugar in cola would also give you a large pot belly.

If you could put up with all these problems, you could probably live on nothing but cola for a long time. However, it is likely that in the end you would go blind, pass into a coma and die of a vitamin deficiency.

By the way, have you ever left a tooth in a glass of cola? Don't try it with your milk teeth, because teeth left in cola will eventually disappear!

MORE COLA, ANYBODY?

How high can an ELEPHANT jump?

There's an old saying:

"I BET YOU CAN'T JUMP HIGHER THAN AN ELEPHANT. I BET I CAN – ELEPHANTS CAN'T JUMP!"

Although some people swear blind they have seen elephants jump, the popular point of view in scientific circles is that they can't.

One thing is certain, elephants don't really need to jump. They have no natural predators, which means that there is nothing that an elephant needs to escape from (apart from human beings who want their tusks, that is). So the ability to run and jump isn't really required.

Adult elephants are immensely strong, which means that they can usually overpower other animals without needing to run away. However, they are also massively heavy (a full-grown African elephant can weigh over six tons), so scientists suspect they simply weigh too much to get airborne.

To jump, an elephant must get all four of its feet off the ground at the same time. To do this from standing still, it would have to bend and straighten its legs quickly, and propel its body upwards off the ground. The muscles and bones in an elephant's legs are not designed for this. They are designed to stay very straight. Even when walking, an elephant sways from side to side, to minimise the amount of bend required in each of its legs.

HOW ABOUT ELEPHANTS MANAGING A RUNNING JUMP?

A study by Stanford University in California, USA, revealed that elephants do seem to run – something that had previously been thought unlikely. The study showed that when elephants are moving quickly (they can reach speeds of over 25 kilometres per hour) their weight bounces up and down. The scientists felt that this 'bouncing' was more like running than walking. However, they believed that the elephants always kept one of their four feet in contact with the ground.

WHAT IF THE ANSWER TO THE QUESTION IS THAT ELEPHANTS ONLY JUMP WHEN NO ONE IS LOOKING?

How does ≫ MEDICINE ≪ make me feel BETTER?

Your body is a staggeringly complicated biological machine — so complicated that some of the amazing things it does are still not fully understood by scientists.

Your body acts as a little factory — taking stuff like food, water and oxygen in and using it to produce the chemicals it needs to work properly. Different organs in your body make different chemicals for different reasons.

When a disease makes one of these functions fail, you may fall ill. Then, your body might produce too much of one chemical, or not enough, or it might send the chemical to the wrong part of your body. For example, some people suffer from an illness called diabetes. This is caused when their bodies have problems making a chemical called 'insulin' which helps to regulate the amount of glucose in their blood. A lack of insulin can make people experience a variety of symptoms, including feeling very tired and thirsty.

As scientists continue to find out what each of the body's organs do, which chemicals the organs make and where those chemicals need to go, they have also been able to work out how to copy the chemicals in laboratories.

A chemical your body requires can be injected straight into your body, or comes in the form of a pill, which you swallow. The pill is digested in your stomach and the chemical (or medicine) gets released into your blood by your liver. Then it travels around the body until it reaches the part of your body that needs it. Once there it will do its job, just as if your body had produced the chemical itself. Hopefully, that solves the problem and makes you feel better. Alternatively, if your body is producing too much of one chemical, a medicine can be used to reduce the amount your body is creating.

Medicine rarely 'cures' an illness. It just replaces or changes a function that your body normally performs on its own. If your body starts working properly again, the doctor may say you can stop taking the medicine. If it doesn't, you have to keep taking the medicine so that your body can stay healthy.

Is there LIFE on other planets?

There is, as yet, no proof that life exists on other planets. No one knows if there are intelligent beings elsewhere in the universe. Scientists don't even know if there are really simple forms of life, like bugs or bacteria, elsewhere in the universe.

Over the years, people have claimed they have seen aliens and flying saucers. Some even say that they have been taken on board alien spaceships, or to distant planets. Scientists, however, have never been able to find any evidence to back up these claims.

The collection of chemicals that make up the Earth, together with its size, density, distance from the Sun, its atmosphere, climate and some other factors, all work together to make the Earth a perfect place for lots of different life forms to exist. It seems unlikely that there is another planet that has all the right ingredients to support life, spinning round another star.

Scientists studying the most likely places that life might be found near Earth — the planet Mars and some of the moons around Jupiter and Saturn — haven't given up looking, but the signs aren't very promising. For over 40 years they have been sending radio signals out into deep space, but, as yet, no one has answered.

None of this means that there is no life out there. The universe contains billions and billions of stars, several billion of which could have a system of planets around them, like our solar system. Some astronomers believe that the sheer size of the universe means that it is likely that there are planets where life has developed in some form.

THE SEARCH CONTINUES ...

In the future, new telescopes should be able to detect the presence of chemicals around planets orbiting nearby stars. They will search the nearest star system to ours, which is called Alpha Centauri. Though it is the nearest star system, Alpha Centauri isn't really very near, being about 41 trillion kilometres away.

The radio signals scientists send out in the hope that an intelligent life form might respond could be replaced with laser-based communications. These signals could be accurately fired out deep into space.

As for the likelihood of aliens visiting our planet, scientists feel the distances are just too huge. Any spaceships coming to Earth would have to travel for years to get here. Even if they came from the nearest star system, Alpha Centauri, and the craft could travel at the speed of light, it would take them 4.3 years to arrive. Human technology is a long way away from developing a craft that can travel that fast, and currently scientists believe that nothing can travel faster than light.

So unless aliens have technology a lot more advanced, than that of human beings, and can travel in ways human beings haven't discovered yet, the chance of meeting an extra-terrestrial being any time soon is very slim.

How do horses SLEEP standing up and not fall over?

How would you like to sleep standing up and not fall flat onto your bum? Just imagine, you could put on a pair of shades and have a nap without anyone even realising what you were doing. Well, sadly for us humans, that's never going to happen, because when we go to sleep our bodies relax far too much.

However, for horses, sleeping and standing at the same time is no problem. They're able to do this because the joints on their legs can lock. This mechanism is called 'stay apparatus', and is an interaction between 'muscles' – the soft tissue that contracts and allows movement, and 'ligaments' – the short bands of tissue that connect two bones. When these ligaments tighten, it allows horses to relax their muscles and rest without falling over.

It's not just horses either – it's common among other four-legged land animals, including elephants, zebras and giraffes. Cows can do this, too, but they usually choose to lie down (lazy cattle).

It might seem strange that an animal would choose to sleep standing up. But animals that do so may actually have an advantage in certain situations. For instance, if they're attacked by a predator they're able to react much more quickly than if they had to lumber to their feet. Also, for large animals such as horses, lying down for too long can restrict blood flow and put pressure on their organs. So standing up is actually good for their health.

However, even horses can't sleep on their hooves all of the time. They must lie down to get a deeper kind of sleep – the kind you get when you go to bed in the evening. They don't need much of it, though! The average horse only sleeps for around three hours within a 24-hour period.

When they do finally drop off, horses use a 'buddy system', where one horse watches over the other horses. This is to protect them from any potential predators lurking in the fields. They rotate around the group so that everyone can get enough deep sleep, until all the horses have had their rest.

What's the WORST smelling thing in the world?

You will probably have your own opinion on what smells horrendous — you might even say your brother's bedroom. It's very much a matter of personal taste, but most people will agree that any list of the most vile-smelling things would include dog poo, vomit, farts, smelly feet, bad breath, and rotting eggs or meat.

When choosing the worst smelling thing in the world, you need to choose something that not only smells bad, but smells very strongly. For this, it is necessary to examine the chemistry of ponginess. Certain chemicals and chemical compounds pop up again and again in bad-smell situations. These include hydrogen sulphide (which makes rotten eggs smell gross) and butyric acid (which lends its distinctive bouquet to some of the riper scented cheeses, sweaty feet and rancid butter).

All of the above smell worse in a laboratory than they do in nature. The merest whiff of a concentrated dose of any of them would have you bringing up your lunch in the blink of a teary eye.

Cadaverine and putrescine are responsible for the smell of dead flesh, and methanethiol is produced by decomposing vegetable matter and adds a cabbagey whiff to farts and bad breath. Titan Arum, also known as the giant corpse flower, is generally agreed to have a smell not unlike a rotting corpse. For this reason, it is probably best avoided as a Mother's Day gift.

But the mother and father of all serious stinks is butyl seleno-mercaptan. This is the stuff that gives the spray produced by a skunk its terrible smell — a smell that clings to things. It's so bad that people who have been hit by the spray often end up burning their clothes to get rid of the pong.

Butyl seleno, and its close relatives ethyl and methyl mercaptan, are so awful that governments have investigated their potential uses for controlling rioting crowds and making military-grade stink bombs. The stench is so powerful that it can be detected even when diluted to two parts in a million. For this reason, tiny amounts are added to odourless natural gas so that leaks can be detected. It is said to smell like a powerful combination of rotting cabbage, garlic, onions, burnt toast and sewer gas.

If I could only eat one food forever, WHICH should I choose?

The human body requires a complex range of proteins, vitamins, minerals and fats to survive.

For this reason, nutritionists recommend you eat a varied diet to make sure you get everything you need. There is probably no single thing you can eat that gives you everything your body needs, but what comes closest?

Some fruits, especially prunes, blueberries and pomegranates, have been found to be particularly good for humans. They contain bags of vitamins and fibre, but also antioxidants. These are chemicals that protect cells in the body from damage.

Acai, a berry found on palm trees in Brazil and the Amazon jungle, may be the world's most nutritious fruit. Containing an impressive collection of healthy vitamins and minerals, protein and fibre, it is also a rich source of amino and fatty acids. These help to slow down the body's ageing process, and might even be a treatment for some cancers. Better still, the berries taste like cherries and chocolate, too!

If you like slimy vegetation, seaweed may be an even better choice than acai berries. It is rich in vitamins and minerals, but also contains more protein than meat and more calcium than milk. Seaweed also helps the body to heal, and keeps your hair and skin healthy. It helps to prevent high blood pressure and boosts your body's resistance to disease and infection. Seaweed has even been found to protect against the effects of pollution and radiation poisoning.

In Japan, people consume a lot of seaweed, and the Japanese live longer and fewer of them suffer from heart disease than people almost anywhere else in the world.

The problem with seaweed is that it contains very few calories, so you'd have to eat a lot of it to get the energy your body needs.

Starchy root vegetables, such as the sweet potato, the Peruvian maca or oriental kudzu, are good all-round foods. Kudzu, for example, has more calories per gram than honey, but the energy you get from it will last a lot longer. It also contains a range of useful vitamins and minerals, and is used to relieve a number of ailments from headaches to chicken pox.

It is possible that you could live quite well on any of these foods, as all of them contain most of the important ingredients you need to live. In time, however, the things they lack – a vitamin missing here, a protein there – would probably have some negative effects on your body. There really is no food in nature that does it all ...

... OR IS THERE?

Bee pollen might be the closest thing in nature to a perfect food. Pollen is the fine powder that flowers produce to fertilise seeds to make new flowers. Bees collect it from flowers. They mix it with their spit and nectar (a sweet liquid also produced by flowers) to make honey. Scientists have studied the possibility of using pollen as a medicine and a food supplement. Athletes use it to boost energy and help them perform better. Records dating back 5,000 years praise its nutritious and healing qualities. Some experts believe that it contains all the necessary nutrients for human survival.

Some nutritionists have stated that, in theory, you could live a healthy life on just bee pollen and water. The only downsides would appear to be a possible allergic reaction (pollen is the stuff that causes hay fever), the difficulty of collecting it (currently achieved by a wire grid with a dish underneath at the door of the beehive), and the fact that the coating around each pollen grain is so tough that it can preserve the contents for a million years. This makes the process of preparing it for eating very expensive.

Which animal is the DEADLIEST in the world?

Mosquitoes kill more people every year than any other animal through spreading malaria and other fatal diseases.

Estimates put the annual death toll from mosquito-carried malaria alone at over 400,000. This is higher than the number of people killed by any other animal. Even human beings with all that military hardware at their disposal don't kill that many people a year.

It's hard to measure one animal against another when it comes to deadliness. Environment is an important factor — the outcome of a fight between a great white shark and a Bengal tiger would depend quite a lot on whether it took place in the Pacific Ocean or the forests of East India.

Sharks and tigers are certainly dangerous, but not all deadly creatures have huge, slavering jaws full of razor-sharp teeth. A poisonous or venomous creature can kill things many times its own size. Over 50,000 people are killed each year by poisonous snakes alone, with the saw-scaled viper topping the table for numbers.

The prize for the creature with the strongest poison probably goes to the golden dart frog. For thousands of years, tribesmen in the South American rainforest where the frogs live have used the poison that covers this frog's skin to tip arrows for hunting and warfare. Just two micrograms of this poison can kill a person. To give you an idea how much that is, there are about six micrograms of ink contained in the full stop at the end of this sentence.

Another contender for World's Most Lethal Creature is the Australian box jellyfish. Its body is only about the size of a salad bowl, but its tentacles (and there are up to 60 of them) can be 4.5 metres long with up to 5,000 stinging cells on each. Just one box jellyfish contains enough venom to kill 60 adult humans. Is this why so many Australians are really good at swimming?

What makes something FUNNY?

Different people laugh at different things, and cultural differences often mean that a sense of humour can be entirely different from one country to the next – so a joke that is hilarious in one place might fall flat in another.

According to a recent scientific study of jokes, British, Irish, Australian and New Zealand audiences like jokes involving word plays and puns, while Americans and Canadians prefer jokes where someone is made to look stupid. Germans laugh at more jokes than anyone else, and Japanese people hardly ever tell jokes at all.

But although humour doesn't always translate, most people seem to laugh three times in particular. Firstly when they feel superior and are pleased with themselves, secondly when they feel relief and stress or tension disappears, and thirdly when they are surprised by something that doesn't make sense.

If someone falls over but is not hurt — by slipping on a banana skin, for example — you might feel relief that they are OK, and also superiority because they look stupid and you didn't fall over.

Part of the scientific study was to try to find the world's funniest joke. Thousands were submitted and people all round the world voted on their favourites. It was won by this entry:

A couple of hunters are out in the woods when one of them falls to the ground. He doesn't seem to be breathing, his eyes are rolled back in his head. The other hunter whips out his mobile phone and calls the emergency services.

'My friend is dead! What can I do?' he gasps to the operator.

'Just take it easy. I can help. First, let's make sure he's dead,' says the operator, in a calm, soothing voice.

There is a silence, then a shot is heard.

The guy's voice comes back on the line. He says:
'OK, now what?'

Scientists conducting the study concluded that the punchline to this joke had all three elements – the superiority over the dumb hunter, the relief of tension and the element of surprise.

It may not be the funniest joke you ever heard, but more people around the world found it funny than any other joke submitted to the study, so the title is deserved!

How do flies WALK across a ceiling?

The first thing to take into account when answering this question is that flies don't weigh very much. Therefore, the pull of gravity on a fly isn't as strong as it is on a person. Still, the fly possesses an impressive range of special equipment which enables it to remain attached to the ceiling while upside down.

Flies' feet each have two pads covered in tiny hairs called 'setae'. The setae are curved and rounded at the ends and act a bit like suction cups, helping the fly to cling on to the ceiling.

The feet produce a mixture of sugars and oils, which results in just enough foot-stickiness to keep the fly in place while still allowing it to walk about.

Each foot also has a pair of tiny claws. These allow the fly to grip microscopic cracks in the ceiling. To make sure the fly doesn't get stuck permanently to a surface, the claws enable it to twist and peel its feet off the ceiling.

A fly usually keeps four of its six feet in contact with a ceiling at all times. That way, it can't walk very fast, but at least two thirds of it is attached at all times, making it less likely to fall.

Flies can walk a lot more quickly when they are the right way up, but to get from one place to another it is quicker for a fly to

... WELL, FLY.

Which is the OLDEST animal in the world?

The main difficulty when answering this question is that it is very hard for scientists to prove an animal's age accurately.

IT REALLY HELPS IF AN ANIMAL HAS BEEN UNDER OBSERVATION ITS WHOLE LIFE.

The oldest chimpanzee in the world was said to be one called Cheeta, who appeared in Tarzan movies in the 1930s. Cheeta was 80 years old when he died in 2011. There might well be older chimps in the jungles of Borneo, but no one knows for sure.

The oldest bird in the world might well be a parrot that belonged to Winston Churchill (Great Britain's prime minister during the Second World War). Charlie, a blue macaw, is thought by his owner to be 118 years old. After 1964, Charlie lived in a pet shop, but he was banned for upsetting the customers by swearing. It seems Churchill had taught Charlie to shout rude things about Adolf Hitler.

Giant Galapagos tortoises are famous for living long lives. There is one, named Harriet, who lived in a zoo in Queensland, Australia. She died in 2006, at the age of 176. 174 years before in 1832, a Seychelles giant tortoise named Jonathan was born. Jonathan is still alive today and is thought to be the oldest currently living terrestrial animal.

The ocean is a good place to be if you want to live a long time. Geoducks (a type of clam) regularly live to about 146. The oldest ever found was 160. Counting the rings on a geoduck's shell is a very reliable way of working out how old it is. To make it to a ripe old age, however, these creatures have to avoid being eaten by humans, cooked with pasta and a nice cream sauce.

Bowheads are a type of whale that have been hunted in the waters around the coast of Alaska for centuries. In 2007, a bowhead whale was found that had a fragment of a weapon embedded in its blubber. The fragment was probably the result of a failed hunting expedition. Experts can date it, quite accurately, back to the 1890s, and this would make the whale between 115 and 130 years old when it died.

The grandaddy of the oceans, however, is generally agreed to be the deep sea tube worm, 'lamellibrachia luymesi'. Lurking at the bottom of the ocean, the worms look a bit like giant lipsticks. Marine scientists can assess the age of the worms from their size and the speed at which they grow. Studies have shown that they can live for up to 250 years, which makes them a good bet for world's oldest animal.

Are Coconuts More Dangerous Than Sharks?
ISBN: 978-1-78055-511-9